FAERY INITIA[TION]

OF
THE THIRTEEN
DREAMERS

A Green Fire Folio

By
Coleston Brown

Published in 2013 by

Le Brun Publications

Canada, Ireland

ISBN-13:   978-0986591259

Cover art and design by Coleston Brown

Book design by Coleston Brown

A Green Fire Folio on the Faery Tradition

Contents

Acknowledgments

I would like to thank Joann Allison, Laurel Bohart, Gil Bourne, Sheila Browning, Mara Freeman, Gill Finleyson, Lorraine Henry, Sue Kearley, Michael Kivinen, Coleen Lane, Yuri Leitch, Addele Lynas, Jackie Queally, Carol Reid, Sue Vincent and Rab Wilkie for venturing to read the initial text of this folio. Special thanks to those who tried the DreamVisions for themselves and offered helpful comments and encouragement. and thanks also to those who helped in ways they may not even have known: in particular Alison Stenning,, "Twilight," George, "the Pixie," Pauline and Alan Royce. Many thanks also to Cliff and Pauline McClinton for ongoing support and encouragement. Deepest gratitude, as always, to my Lady, Faery Artist Jessie Skillen, for for her love and support, and for much helpful advice on the design and selection of images, including several of her own inspired works.

Author's Note

This Folio is, in some respects, a full-colour supplement to my *Secrets of a Faery Landscape: new light on the Glastonbury Zodiac* (Green Fire, May 2012). Abridged versions of the text and DreamVisions also appeared in *Signs and Secrets of the Glastonbury Zodiac:An Anthology by the Maltwood Moot* edited by Yuri Leitch and published by Avalonian Aeon Publications (April, 2013). New textual material in this Folio includes, but is not limited to, a section on the Thirteen Dreamers as Immortal Presences, expanded and new practical forms, and additional commentary on the DreamVisions.

To make the best use of the material presented here, I suggest reading the entire folio through before trying the practical work. When you do begin to work practically with the material you will find helpful my audio CD entitled **The Faery Oath of Friendship,** which presents the DreamVisions and oath with accompanying music on the Celtic Zither. This method of learning provides a useful bridge between modern written presentation and a more traditional bardic style of oral transmission of deeply transformative imagery.

Introduction

n the first few weeks following the publication of my book: *Secrets of a Faery Landscape: new light on the Glastonbury Zodiac* (Green Fire Publications, May 2012). I had a series of powerful dreams apparently generated by my magical connections to the land around Glastonbury Somerset. These DreamVisions came in the form of a magical journey and culminated in a final DreamVision in which I was given, almost word-for-word, a Faery Oath of Friendship. These dream journeys and ritual oath have since become an important component of my magic-spiritual practice. I have shared them with a number of people who have remarked on their regenerative, inspirational effects. It occurs to me that others might also benefit from this work. However, before setting out the gist of these visions and the Faery Oath, I first present an overview of the dynamics involved in Faery initiation,.

The following includes material adapted from my aforementioned book.

Stars, Landscape, & Faery Initiation

he stars and landscape are closely bound up with Faery Initiation. Faery Initiation is an experience of personal regeneration and rebirth that arises from a direct relationship with the landscape and the presences and powers within it.

Certain Celtic traditions tell how Faery presences descended from the stars into the earth. These traditions are reflected in later Christianised tales such as that in Wolfram von Eschenbach's *Parzival*, where the hermit Trevrizent tells how the Grail was written in the stars and how it was brought down to earth by "neutral angels."(*Book 9*) We have here a theme or motif that is well-documented world-wide ~ the descent of sacred mysteries from the celestial region, the OverRealm, which is the spiritual zone associated with powers and presences in their most primal expression.

All over the world, imposing or important landforms are commonly associated with deities, heroes, and other sacred presences who are also connected to constellations, stars, planets, moon, sunrise, sunset, and so on. The transforming effect of these presences and landforms on the health and harmony of the people and creatures that live in the surrounding landscape is undeniable.

For instance, when I moved to Vancouver Island, Canada in 2007, I discovered there were tales of divine beings descending from the stars into the landscape, merging with hills, rivers, stones and trees. Right behind my home I could see a series of ridges which together form what is locally known as the "sleeping shaman."

Faery Initiation also rests at the core of the Hermetic and related traditions, most notably the Alchemical and Rosicrucian currents, after an engraving by Michael Maier in *Symbola Aureae Mensae duodecim nationum* (1617)

The Sleeping Shaman   © 2013 by Coleston Brown

This figure is the ancestral Dreamer of the local Salish tribe near Ladysmith, British Columbia. What is remarkable about this particular example is that it reflects a living tradition, still active and still actively engaged by the aboriginal peoples who have lived in the area for thousands of years. During my time there I considered it a great opportunity and a blessing to be part of this sacred landscape and to be able to forge significant relationships with it. In the ensuing years I have relocated from Canada to the west of Ireland, Although physically Eire is a world away, I find myself ensconced in a similarly resonant magical atmosphere. In Canada I lived in the shadow of a great male sleeper in the mountain, and here my entire horizon is filled with a series of hills and mountains, which viewed from a distance, outline the reclining body of the the Morrigan— great triple goddess of the *Tuatha de Danaan*— whose mythological lore fills and enlivens the local landscape and those who dwell within.

Faery Initiation also rests at the core of the Hermetic and related traditions, most notably the Alchemical and Rosicrucian currents, which are concerned with the celestial powers inside the earth. These are the key to the transformation and regeneration of mortal beings and of matter itself.

Shamanic tradition also bears many Faery elements— from vision quests to faery marriages.

It is important to realise that Faery Initiation is not any sort of solemn ceremony é dramatically performed by humans é and it cannot be transmitted by any mortal power. All we humans can do is act as a bridge and mediate the Faery Initiation. Significantly, Faery Initiation is usually mediated through a a member of the opposite sex. This is because of deep issues of faery-human polarity and interaction. This transmission or awakening, passed male to female or female to male, reflects dynamics found among traditional Faery Doctors here in the west of Ireland, who are obliged, even today, to

In 1925 Katharine Emma Maltwood, working in Chilton Priory, her strange, towered abode, looked over the landscape near Glastonbury, Somerset. She was getting a feel for the map she had been commissioned to produce for a new edition of Sebastian Evans' translation of *The High History of the Holy Grail*.
As she pondered the curious appearance of a lion in the story, she had a flash of vision and saw the figure of a great feline shaped in the hills and hollows of the countryside before her. She later associated this figure with the ancient constellation of Leo.

pass on ther particular "Cure" to someone of the opposite sex. (this pattern is carried through in the work presented below.)

Faery Initiation works off of two main lines of contact or transmission. These are the lines of sacred space(which includes the beings who inhabit that space) and sacred lore, both of which are bound up with the mystery of the Three Realms and with sacred geography and the inherent power of a locality. The Glastonbury Faery Ring, by both design and nature, constitutes an initiatic centre or focus of spiritual power and presence. It is a place of initiation, transformation and regeneration both of people and of streams of sacred lore As Katharine Maltwood herself realised, the entire complex is "a symbol of a secret cycle and Initiation". (*Enchantments of Britain* P35). I suggest that this secret cycle and initiation is of Faery.

Thus her awareness of stellar correlations arose directly out of her contact with great presences in the landscape and the deep earth. The land spoke to her and revealed the secrets of the stars and the meaning of sacred lore. This is not a result of stories having been being consciously "mapped" on the landscape, but of the land revealing its mysteries through sacred lore, including its interrelationships with stellar and chthonic or UnderRealm powers and presences.

All the motifs and magical themes of esoteric traditions rise out of these interrelationships and take on forms of expression that are meaningful and regenerative for the people inhabiting a landscape. All coherent traditions of sacred lore stem from the interaction of human consciousness with the powers and presences of the landscape, atmosphere and stars.

The Glastonbury Faery Ring is an empowered place, largely natural, partly modelled, that epitomises and embodies the primal sacred landscape, the Earth of Light, Land of Immortality, or Region of the Summer Stars. As a fusion of the celestial patterns and powers of the OverRealm with the chthonic powers and centralising light of the UnderRealm, it is an area particularly open to initiatic forces. For those already on the magical path, being in the Circle is like being in a living temple or sacred space. Power flows instantaneously and effectively into consciousness allowing for important inner work to be done.

This power is also available, in some degree, to anyone who lives in or has visited the sacred area. Bear in mind,

For Katharine Maltwood the sacred landscape around Glastonbury, Somerset inspired the mysteries and legends of the Quest for the Holy Grail ~*The Grail Knight, Frederick J.Waugh ~ 1921*

however, that this merely makes an opportunity available, it doesn't guarantee a faery initiation. There must always be present certain preconditions or requisites for the faery initiation to manifest, the most fundamentally important of which is a certain awareness and openness to the "Stream" and the wonders of a life of magic and enchantment.

The Thirteen Dreamers

... I first launched forth on my voyage of discovery to "the Land of the Giants", and found them lying asleep in a circle ...

-- **King Arthur's Round Table** *of the Zodiac* (Maltwood, 1946, p. 24)

Faery Dreamers are found the world over, and hold an important place in sacred lore. But the immortal Dreamers of Somerset have a special significance for our own era, which is one reason Glastonbury and environs has retained its significance as a spiritual centre. Since such presences express and to an extent form the landscape in which they rest, we find them often linked with local lore.

This is in fact, just how the Somerset Faery Dreamers were

The High History of the Holy Grail (Perlesvaus), an Old French Arthurian romance dating to the first decade of the 13th century, may have been written at Glastonbury Abbey (above).

first "discovered" by Katharine Maltwood in 1925 when she was absorbed in making a map connecting the local landscape around Glastonbury with the lore recorded in a work known as the High History of the Holy Grail. This tale, first written down circa 1200 AD, demonstrated knowledge of the area and placed there the quest of King Arthur and the Knights of the Round Table for Th.e Holy Grail.

Mrs Maltwood quickly realised however that the tales of the Grail knights were Christian reincarnations of more ancient Celtic mysteries of the UnderRealm and the Stars imaged in the landscape. Yet strangely enough these more ancient expressions are not always easy to locate in her work where they are camouflaged by later Arthurian legend on the one hand and numerous diversions and digressions on the other. This and her unfortunate tendency to seek the key to the area in Middle-Eastern mythology and in spurious historical influences have confused and confounded many who have sought to understand her works. Nonetheless, throughout her books and papers, we find references to "Nature gods" and "Giants" two terms that were often used by 19th and early 20th century scholars to describe Faery beings (most notable in this regard are the treatments given the Tuatha da Danann and the Irish *sidhe* in general). The primal material underlying the entire Star Temple , Landscape, or Faery Ring includes the secret of the ancient Celtic star forms and the

Faery Dreamers in the land.

By its very nature a Faery Landscape has the capacity to find expression in the imaginations of those who

Faery Landscape This outline first appeared in my *Secrets of a Faery Landscape.* It is worth replicating here as it throws light on the kinds of energies and influences encountered in the

It is here that the desire wakens to seek the way of Caer Sidhe and the Cauldron of Inspiration and Regeneration. The Quest also has a manifestation inside the circle in the figure of the

Encounter with a faery, *George W. Russel (A.E.) ~ 1919*

live and move within it. This accounts for the tendency of the powers in the land to take various forms and images, and to accrue to various mythologies and other forms of sacred lore. With this deep root material in mind, I present below an outline of the Thirteen Dreamers of the Somerset

DreamVisions presented later in this Folio.

1. **The Quest:** This Dreamer dreams the sense of a quest, awakening the Seeker.. The Quest may appear as a Cu Sidhe, a Faery hound or a wild boar or sow.

little dog that accompanies the Child. In Welsh lore, this Dreamer is particularly associated with faery hounds such as *Dormath*, the hound of Gwyn ap Nudd, and *Drudwyn* who with Mabon ap Modron hunted the "questing beast" in the form of a wild boar.

2. The Queen: The Queen of Faery dreams forth the powers of fertility, sovereignty, birth and death. She appears as mother, lover, maiden, enchantress, warrior and witch. She is associated in particular with flowing waters such as springs, rivers and streams, and often appears in connection with Cauldrons, dragons and serpents. She is also linked with crows and swans.

In Celtic Myth her presence is expressed through figures such as the Welsh Don, Cerridwen, Modron, Creiddylad, and the Irish triple goddess the Morrigan. These presences are closely related to the later Arthurian figures of Morgan La Fey, Gwenevere and the Lady of the Lake, who together assume many of the attributes of the Queen of Faery.

3. The King: The Faery King dreams the powers of generation and regeneration, rulership, seeding and seeking, harmony and conflict, shape-shifting and strength. He appears often as father, hunter and warrior-bard. We find him connected especially with hills and high places, and also horses, hounds, swans, and dragons.

In Celtic myth, the King manifests through figures like the Welsh Arawn, Gwynn ap Nudd, and the Irish Dagda. He is also associated with Taliesin, Avalach, the Celtic Apollo and, in later tradition, with King Arthur.

4. The Radiant Child: Dreams the powers of prophecy, union of opposites and conjoining complementary energies, innocence, balance, new life, and beginnings.

The Faery Child may appear male, female or androgynous. May alternate between infant and ancient. Sometimes appears as star or leaf faced, or in the form of a hare. The Child is the Faery Emissary, and of considerable importance here because the Faery Ring as a whole is impressed with a body of sacred lore and stellar power relating particularly to the bringing forth of a Child of Light from the UnderRealm.

In Celtic tradition the Child appears as Mabon ap Modron (Son of the Mother), Gwydion and Taliesin, Aengus the Ever-Young, the child Fionn, and also as the young Brigid.

5. The Faery Boat: Dreaming the Journey. The Faery Boat is a magical, enchanted means of travel along the glimmering stream of DreamVision. It often appears as a living faery vessel --with or without a sail -- that moves of its own accord or is propelled by a faery wind. It is connected with the Welsh/British coracle and the Irish currach, both of which are traditional boats made of woven willow and covered with animal skins (usually deer or horse). The currach is larger than the coracle and more often fitted with one or two sails.

6. The Havens: this is the dreaming of the tidal port, the harbour into the Realm of Faery. It is a place of transition and a threshold of Faery Initiation.

The Haven Master may appear as a faery being who bears scissors, comb and mirror, and blows a ramís horn to pilot boats in through the faery mist. In Celtic lore he may be associated with the Welsh Manawydan fab Llŷr and the Irish Manannan Mac Lir whose faery flocks of sheep appear as mist.

In Celtic lore the currach and coracle appear often, especially in connection with Mannanan. In Welsh lore, the infant Taliesin is found in a coracle. And in later Arthurian tales, Morgan le Fay bears Arthur to Avalon in a magic boat.

7. The Sisterhood: This is the dreaming of the faery women, and is linked particularly to the moon and tides, the magic of the ninth wave, and the powers of inspiration and visioning the directions. The Sisterhood is found most often as seven and/ or nine faery maidens, lovers, sisters, witches or deer priestesses. Numerous tales of sisterhoods of seven or nine women occur throughout Celtic lore.In Welsh myth we have the nine maidens whose breath warms the Cauldron of Inspiration. In Irish myth, the Morrigan appears with nine braids in her hair,

and is said to have the sexual power of seven women.8 In Arthurian legend there is a group of nine women consisting of Morgan le Fey and her eight sisters — shape-shifters and healers who live on the Isle of Avalon.

8. The Faery Cat: The Faery Cat dreams the powers of nobility, independence, courage and the raising of the inner fire. This presence most often appears as a lynx or a large black wildcat with a white spot on its breast. Legends of the Faery Cat are known in Scotland (*Cat Sith*) ,Wales (*Cath Palug*), and Ireland (*Cait Sidhe*). In Arthurian lore, the Faery Cat often appears in the form of a lion.

9. The Faery Stone: The living Stone dreams forth from the Source sigils and Faery runes. The latter may appear as Ogham or with unknown Faery signs that can be seen to play upon and flow beneath the surface of the Stone. They respond when you touch or even look upon them, awakening a deep feeling and emotional awareness of all that is particularly valuable for you. Most often this Dreamer appears as a tall standing

stone with moss and faery sigils and other carvings on it. The Dreamer an also appear as a stream of sigils or faery signs flowing across the land like a river of silvery blue-green light.

In myth and sacred geography we have the Celtic "Stones of Destiny," such as the Lia Fáil of Irish tradition and the Scottish Stone of Scone. In Arthurian legend we have

The Faery Stone © 2007 by Coleston Brown.

the siege perilous — a standing stone gifted to Arthur by the Faery.

10. The Horned One: The Horned or Antlered One dreams the thresholds of time, and light, the powers of path-finding, nature in general, animals, and sexual energy. The Antlered One is the guardian of the "gate of the Deities, which may be associated with the winter solstice". Sometimes appears as a stag or a deer, or an antlered man or woman, but also sometimes as a hag. In Celtic lore the Horned One appears most often in the guise of Cernunnos, and the Cailleach, especially in her form as deer Goddess.

11. **The Faery Bird:** The Faery Bird dreams the centre and the turning of great cycles of time, as well as the ability to cross thresholds of reality. Most often this Dreamer appears as a swan, goose, raven or eagle, which drinks from a well on a sacred mound or hill. In Celtic

Glastonbury Faery Swan. © 2012 by Jessie Skillen

lore it is associated with any of the Swan Maidens, the Crow woman or with Aengus Og or Mabon/Maponus the Celtic Apollo. In Celtic tradition this Dreamer signifies the centre of or entrance to Avalon, the Realm of Faery and the UnderRealm.

12. The Faery Fish: The Faery Fish dreams the visions of the deep, movement, return to the Source, sacrifice and regeneration. Appearing most often as a salmon, or seal, this Dreamer instils a sense of wisdom, dedication, sacrifice and inspired awareness. In Celtic lore the Faery Fish is associated with the Salmon of Knowledge, the Faery Child, and the many myths and legends of selkies and mermaids.

13. The Faery Well or Well of Stars: The Well dreams the source of stars within the Earth, and thus enables, mirrors and completes the power of the Blood Well in the Dreamer of the Faery Bird. The Dreamer of the Well May appear as three ghostly maidens or Faery women, or as a triad of swan, dragon and faery

hill. This presence sometimes appears as or with a harp. In this the Well resonates closely with the Dreamer of the Faery Bird. In Celtic tradition holy wells and sacred pools appear often, as do whirlpools — all of which extend into the image of the Cauldron of Inspiration and Plenty and the Faery Glass or mirror-pool reflecting the stars.

The Dreamers dream within the earth and stars, awaiting mortal awareness to enliven their visions. Those whose spiritual destiny and calling is to mediate between the Worlds are in a special position to bring this pattern to life and realization.

Immortal Presences

The Thirteen Immortal Dreamers are great Faery presences within the landscape of Somerset, but they are also OtherWorld contacts with a spiritual stream of their own and thus may be met or encountered anywhere. They may manifest through features in any local landscape or through local custom, legend or myth.

Thus we find that the Child often appears in connection with trees, the King with hills, The Faery Queen with bodies of water, and so on. Hills in particular are common points of contact for all the Dreamers—hence the worldwide occurrence of the motif of "the hollow hills." (a similar observation could be made with regard to sacred Islands. Because they are in the landscape, The Immortals are both hidden and visible, seen and unseen, and thus accessible in the green place of even the busiest cities.

In several respects the Thirteen Immortal Dreamers resemble the Eight Immortals of Chinese Daoist Tradition. For instance:

1. both are groups of Exemplary presences in a recognised stream of tradition in which they are associated with specific myths, legends and other forms of Sacred Lore.

2. they are both contacted by magical practitioners for help and protection.

3. Both are associated with hills and sacred Islands.

4. Both are linked to a celestial boat or faery ship that sails them through the heavens..

The Eight Daoist Immortals sailing the Heavens in their boat .

The Faery Ship © 2007 by Coleston Brown.

The Faery Landscape & the Maltwood Zodiac

The teachings on the somerset Faery Landscape are developments of the initial visions and realisations of Katharine Maltwood circa 1925. These Faery revelations account for much in Mrs Maltwood's initial vision that has otherwise been misunderstood — perhaps not least by herself! For the sake of reference, I include here the major correspondences between the Thirteen Dreamers and the more accepted layout of the effigies of the Glastonbury Zodiac as presented by Mrs Maltwood in her works:

1. The Quest. This corresponds with Maltwood's Two Dogs

2. The Havens corresponds with Aries.

3. The Sisterhoods relate to Taurus, the Pleiades and Hyades.

4. The Faery Child, resonates powerfully with

Gemini, Lepus the Hare and Orion.

5. The Faery Queen corresponds to Virgo.

6. The King corresponds to Sagittarius the Archer, and Hercules.

7. The Horned One corresponds to Capricorn.

8. The Faery Bird/ swan corresponds to Aquarius.

9. The Faery Cat or Lynx connects to Cancer and Leo.

10. The Stone corresponds to Scorpio.

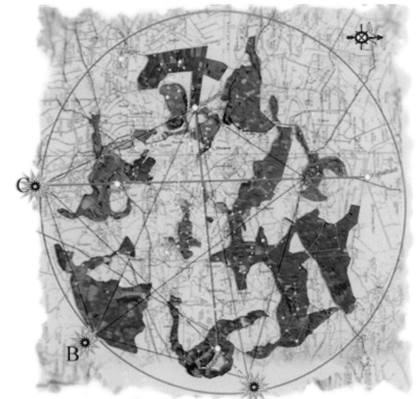

Power Alignments of Stellar Fire in the Glastonbury Enclosure. The three solstice points are A) Conceiving of powers, B) Sunrise/Birth, C) Transit/ Illumination.

The !3 Dreamers in the landscape of Somerset. © 2007 by Coleston Brown

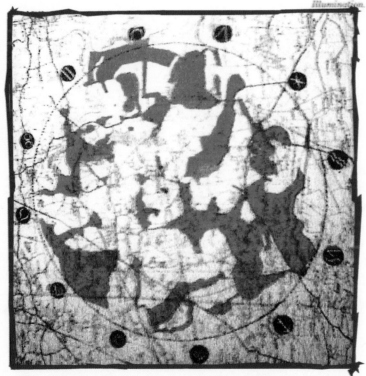

The !3 effigies in the lanscape of Somerset. 1934? by Katharine Maltwood, Photo © Coleston Brown 2008.

11.The Faery Fish connects to Cetus and Pisces.

12.The Faery Boat relates to The Ship, Argo Navis.

13.The Well of Stars/ Light, corresponds with Maltwoodís "3 points" at the centre of the Circle and her "Enclosure of the Sun" containing Ursa Major and Ursa Minor, Lyra (the Harp), Cygnus and Draco.

These are of course rough comparisons, but useful in that they allow us to relate various other presentations of the Glastonbury Star Enclosure to the various presences of the Immortal Dreamers.

The Dreamers dream within the earth and stars, waiting for their visions to be enlivened by mortal awareness. Those whose spiritual destiny and calling is to mediate between the Realms are in a special position to bring this pattern to life and realisation.

> Walkers of the Levels of Light, let us cast a Vision, let us open to a Sacred Place, a place within the Primal Pattern hidden in the landscape of our outer world.
>
> Yet let not Vision come through sight alone, the whole of being is in play here, so also listen, feel, and sense the way. We are about to go upon a journey ~ a journey into DreamVision…

The Dream Visions & the Oath

Below is a version of the Dream-Vision material that inspired this Folio. This work is a way of attuning to the initiatory powers of the Thirteen Dreamers of the Somerset Faery Ring/Star Temple and of pledging to Faery in general as friend, advocate and mediator. The DreamVisions are presented in a deliberately condensed, direct style that I have developed over the years in my workshops and teaching. It has proven a highly effective way of presenting magical imagery.

The practical work given below are intended as a guide only, and is capable of considerable development in light of your own insights and magical experience.

DreamVision I

…You stand on a grass-covered hill of red earth that rises like a small island from a mist-covered lake. You realise the red earth to contain the spirits of the ancestors and the green grass the essence of Faery. These you sense might manifest at any moment through the mist …. The mist swirls before you in resonance to a power you sense stirring in the land — like a whirling spiral

of wisdom~ the wisdom of the ancestors. You feel their awareness rising in your blood, an arousal or awakening that transforms your own consciousness; their powers merge with yours and your minds conjoin as living streams of knowledge and peace that whirl and turn and sparkle and shine like streams of stars within the womb of inner Earth and within your being.

You are aware that they are integrating their being with yours. You now *See* ~ both as yourself in the contemporary world and as your forebears did. You are able to embrace the landscape and to participate in its mystery and power in ways you never before realised. You feel a sense of anticipation building as if a door to another world was about to open …. and so it is….

Peace to all Powers.

Be all in Peace within,

Peace to all Powers

Be all in Peace without,

Deep Peace To All

DreamVision 2

… A small,single-masted coracle or curragh with a green mast and a red sail approaches through the mist, guided by a great silver-scaled Salmon. In the coracle are the Faery Child, a Lynx and a small white hound, while a kingfisher perches on the mast. These are the animal helpers or allies of

the faery child. The Child being a faery child is of indeterminate sex and age, sometimes appearing very young, sometimes very old, but always exudes joy and wisdom.You may even feel exuberant, even a little giddy when the presence of the FaeryChild is near,especially at first, but this is fairly common and no cause for concern.

In the boat with TheFaery Child are a Lynx ,a small white dog, and a kingfisher…..

Peace to all Powers.

Be all in Peace within,

Peace to all Powers

Be all in Peace without,

Deep Peace To All

DreamVision 3

…A second white hound-- this one massive and red- eared --bounds past us to greet the coracle and its occupants...
The great hound barks and yelps leaping enthusiastically back and forth between us and the sparkling shoreline as the coracle glides to a standstill crunching onto the foamy shingle and shells. The massive

houndís enthusiasm is so infectious that we are drawn by its playful invitations to come down to the sea and climb aboard the little magical vessel...

As the last amongst us sits down gently within, we hear and feel the booming note of a great horn reverberating across the waves. It carries a faery wind in its sonorous tones. The horn and wind bring a deep sense of anticipation,and longing upon us. The Great hound bays in response to the horn. Our sail billows slightly and we move slowly off into the mist. Wisps of faery fog float here and there before us and were reminded of the ancient tales that speak of such apparitions as "Manannan's lambs." The Horn sounds once more, its powerful, ancient note accompanied by a second faery wind, which immediately fills the little red sail and, with a thrill that runs like electricity through us, grips our little coracle as though in an invisible hand and propels us swiftly far from shore and out onto the foam-crested waves and into the watery wilds...

The Havens © 2012 by Jessie Skillen.

Flashes of silver here and there remind us that we are guided by a sacred salmon—the salmon of knowledge — who knows the hidden ways of faery and the secret streams and currents in the sea and aligns our little craft with the tides that rise and fall with the moon. All these affect our course and carry us towards an unknown shore. Anticipation and longing rise again strong within us as we pass between the worlds...

Peace to all Powers.

Be all in Peace within,

Peace to all Powers

Be all in Peace without,

Deep Peace To All

And All Be Well.

DreamVision 4

...We glide silently across the sea in our magic boat. The power of the great horn still resonates within us and in the air, vibrating through every part of the coracle ~ from the rudder-paddle to the tip of the green mast, seeming to add new gusts of enchanted wind to the sail as needed. A natural harbour seems to manifest out of the misty waves. A semi-circular line of Faery boats are drawn up along the shore, each moored to the trunk of a willow tree. We ride up onto the shore, disembark, and are met by the Ram-headed, green-cloaked, Harbour Master. This is Mananan, the Faery King of the Sea and mist, Lord of the Havens.

He secures our boat to a sigil-inscribed willow tree with a length of Faery cord~ triple-braided in red, white and green to reflect the triple threads of influence that initiate and activate our quest. The Haven Master looks at each of us searchingly, speaking to us in deep soft tones, as he presents us each with a small, round mirror of dark-coloured glass and a magic knife having a sharp, finely-worked blade of hawthorn wood. We get back into our boat, carefully tucking away our faery glass and hawthorn blade. The Haven Master unties our craft, rolls up the magic cord and hands it to the

Faery Child. Mananan removes a horn from his head and blows a loud blast, sending the faery wind into the crimson sail. We glide swiftly out onto the foam-crested waves remembering the words spoken to us by the Lord of the Havens...

Peace to all Powers.

Be all in Peace within,

Peace to all Powers

Be all in Peace without,

Deep Peace To All....

And All Be Well.

DreamVision 5

...We are in the small craft, having just come from our meeting with the Havens Master. The Mist begins to lift off the lake as the sun rises into the sky behind us and in the distance we can see the green silhouette of the coastline. The scales of the salmon of knowledge glint in the sunlight as the great fish bobs and weaves smoothly through the water before us. In time, the salmon guides us into a narrow river.

...We come to a stone bridge crossing the river.

There is a narrow stair leading from the river bank up to the bridge As we near the bank the Child transforms into a golden hare and leaps out of the boat and up the stairs, The Lynx and hounds give chase.

We, of a sudden, become concerned and bound after them. But we find The Child and its companions playing together at the mossy base of a great standing stone

The stone is finely carved with runes and sigils, which come alive as we grow near. The sigils on the stone include the true name of the Faery Child and our own faery names. These become

Salmon of Wisdom © 2007 by Coleston Brown.

illumined as we touch the stone.   they flow in a stream from the stone~ green and phosphorescent, with flashes of red and white. The sigil-stream flows on down the bank to the river, entering the water just in front of where our coracle is moored. The salmon darts and plays among them. ..... The golden hare transforms back into a child and leads us down the stair and into the coracle...

Peace to all Powers.

Be all in Peace within,

Peace to all Powers

Be all in Peace without,

Deep Peace To All

And All Be Well.

DreamVision 6

...Our little boat sails off along the stream of swirling sigils that now fill the water.

In a green wave ,the sigils rise into the sky, bearing our coracle up and away with it. The shimmering, flashing green sigils change into cobalt blue butterflies. Among the myriads of butterflies we discern also the kingfisher like a blue streak darting and whirling about our coracle . Other birds join in the joyous flight, singing and calling as they go. As we are lifted up. butterflies and birds turn into stars and Presences.We recognise in their singing, the ancient traditions of the 'Language of Birds" , also known as the "Green Tongue" and the "Language of Stars," said to be the mystical language of paradise, of faery and angel, the true, rhythmic language of scripture, prayer, ritual, recitation, charm and augury, and we feel own inherent powers of foresight, farsight, and understanding of deep things awakening to new life within us as we travel along the shining Dream-path of stars and Presences.we begin to descend towards the earth

and realise our coracle is borne once again by birds and blue butterflies.

These magical creatures carry our wee boat securely and gently lay it down on a wooded hill...... We still hear the mystical "Language of the birds" which seems to say....

Peace to all Powers.

Be all in Peace within,

Peace to all Powers

Be all in Peace without,

Deep Peace To All

DreamVision 7

...A pavilion of green brocade is before us in the wooded glade where we have come to rest in our magic coracle.

We disembark and enter the richly furnished pavilion - we each find a place to settle round a

large table well stocked with rich dishes, fruits,berries, unearthly plants and vegetables and copious flagons of drink. In the background, we hear beautiful music ~ a faery melody that grows all the sweeter as the Faery King and Queen enter the pavilion, each riding on the back of a wild deer.

The King takes out a small harp and plays a sparkling faery tune and the Faery Queen begins to sing a wondrous song of life that fills us with the most incredible sense of joy.

When their song is over, the king and Queen leave and the Faery Child motions us to follow. A group of women gather round us and transform into wild deer. We climb onto their backs and they carry us as part of the royal entourage through the forest and far up into mountainous wilds.

Here on a mountain peak we see the Great Goddess of wells and weaving. She is many-armed and weaves together rainbows and Starlight into destinies, which ,once spun She casts into the centre of the landscape below.

The Faery Hare © 2013 by Jessie Skillen. *see also page 32*

We acknowledge Her and Her power as the deer carry us away and down towards a tall hill that rises gracefully from the surrounding marshland. We skirt the hill and on another rise come to a holy well-spring. Its waters run blood red into a deep pool. In its unfathomable depths we see the glint and shimmer of our old companion The salmon. He seems to grow brighter and rise to the surface, as if called by our gaze. As his silvery back breaks the surface of the pool, scales become feathers as he transforms into a swan and the magical pool becomes a wide still lake. The swan grows enormous and as it fills our view, it bends its neck and carefully lifts us in its beak and onto its great snowy back. .Safe in his feathers we soar together into the sky, up through the clouds and through the blue and pale veils between sky and space. The swan transforms into a great white dragon and we sit back against the ridge scales of its back. It is as though we are in great chairs turning slowly upon the starry winds of space.. Far away beneath us, we see the Faery Landscape of Somerset and the figures of the

Thirteen Dreamers dreaming within it.

The dragon makes one final turn and we slip from our Uneasy Chairs, falling towards the Well of Light at the centre of the Ring of Dreams, where we land lightly in a five-pointed clearing in a wood.

The child takes out the magic Faery mirror, the three colour triple faery cord and the hawthorn blade— gifts from the

Harbour Master. And we do the same, taking out our blade and mirror. And looking in the mirror we see within the face of the Child, but in the opposite sex to our own. If we are male we see a female reflection looking back at us, and if female we see a male featured child within the glass.. The Child grows older and the reflection of their face merges with our own. The face we now see is that of our Faery Other. As we recognise each other, the Child/Other takes out their Hawthorn Blade and cuts a length of the three-coloured Faery cord. With it, they bind our left hand to their right hand. Then the Faery Child speaks a sacred oath of Friendship which we repeat back line by line.

The Oath

I bind myself:
My hand to your hand,
My mind to your mind,
My heart to your heart .
I bind myself:
By the power of Three times three
All within you
all within me
I bind myself:
by the sacred Triple Cord of Red, and White, and Green.

By Starry sky and land and sea,
By oak and ash and Faery Tree
I bind myself:
By King and Queen and Emissary,

I Pledge my self to be
true friend of faery and the Thirteen Dreams
stars within earth
Earth within stars
Peace to all Powers
Light on all Ways
Mortal and immortal,
Bound together
Reborn forever,
In the name of the Radiant Child of Faery
Let it be so, and all be well.
* * * * *

Notes and Comments on the Visions & Faery Oath

In my dream awareness I knew the red earth contained the minds of the Ancestors and the green grass, the essence of Faery. The white mist signifies the Spirit Realm where all worlds and beings meet.

The Salmon
is the Celtic Salmon of Knowledge. The oldest remains of a Lynx in Britain were discovered in Gough's Cave in the Mendip Hills overlooking the Somerset Levels.

The Two Hounds
are *Dormarth*, the great Hound of Gwyn ap Nudd and *Drudwyn*, the hunting hound of Mabon, the celtic Child of Light

The Harbour Master is
Faery king of the seas and master of the winds with his magical horn .

Mananan's Gifts

Mirror:
In my dream this appeared as a round faery glass with a five pointed star engraved in it. No doubt this is linked to the Apple Star pattern of ley lines active in the land, and closely connected to the birth of the Faery Child on the Winter solstice s in the current phase of our present era. (See *Secrets of a Faery Landscape* for more on this incredible event, now unfolding.)

The Hawthorn Blade
is a faery knife or Trow sword that has magical applications.

The Triple Faery Cord
is another artefact with many applications. The three colours , red, green and white signify the three streams that run through spiritual tradition; Ancestral, Faery and Spirit Streams respectively. The same three colours are hinted at in the stream of sigils which sparkle and flash red and white within the flowing green wave.

The Stream of Sigils

Those inscribed on the stone include the true name of the Faery Child and our own faery names-é these become illumined as we touch the stone.

The blue butterflies suggest this dream is linked to Collard Hill.

The Green Pavilion is
a place of healing and gathering. It grew in importance in a further set of visions having to do with the Healing Armour of the Faery Knights of the Green Mantle; wherein magical green armour of energy is gifted by a young female blacksmith (associated with Brigid), who fits and adjusts the various pieces of armour to your energetic body. It has the power to heal and strengthen the area it is made for (see inset).

The Deer Priestesses,
together with a group of seven swan maidens comprise the two sisterhoods- they need only be called upon for help , for it to manifest in our lives.

The horned many armed goddess of wells, whirlpools and weaving is an aspect of the Goddess as crone or Cailleach. In my original dream, the destinies she spins are those of the inner company of spirits journeying together.

The Healing Armour of the Knights of the Green Mantle ~ a DreamVision

The following DreamVision can be entered into regularly.

1. Open a sacred space around you.

2. You recline on a bed in a green pavilion.

3. A white hound enters the tent, and licks your hand to rouse you.

4. A smithy girl enters bearing pieces of armour made of green light.

5. She dresses you in pearlescent mail, then

6. fits each piece of green-light armour to your body, beginning with the feet.

7. As each piece is fitted you feel healing energy, power and protection entering you being on all levels from physical to spiritual.

8. When the helmet is placed upon you the Queen enters with attendants. She ties her scarf to your helmet, the attendants come forward and place a green cloak over your shoulders.

9. The queen dubs you a knight of the green mantle, and you feel the power and healing energy of the armour coursing through you.

10. Meditate on this as long as you need...

11. Give thanks and close the space.

12. Be aware of the Armour throughout the day as needed.

The Holy Spring is the red spring of Chalice Hill. In my dream, the draon shifted from white to red to green.

The Uneasy Chair is a reflection of the initiatory chair of the great Bard, Taliesin as recorded in the *Hanes Taliesin*

In my original dream we land gently in an area that contains our destiny as woven by the Goddess on her vast starry spindle and flung wide into the landscape.

Faery Other: The Faery Other should not be confused with the Faery Co-walker ,which latter is generally of the same sex as you. Strange and unhealthy liaisons have resulted from such a confusion. It has been known for instance for a mortal man or

woman to fall in love with another person's co-walker, resulting in a romance founded entirely on faery enchantment and inappropriate psychological projections.

Page 25, The Horned Woman, Weaver of Destinies. © 2012 by Jessie Skillen.

Entering The Deep Peace & Opening The Directions

It is useful, before embarking upon visionary work, to spend a few minutes emptying oneself of the stress and distractions gathered during the course of daily life. One method of doing this is through a practice known as "emptying the directions." Begin by sitting or lying comfortably, breathing in a steady, gentle rhythm. Be aware of the attunement of your entire being to your breath, and recall that the breath signifies the stream of Spirit through you. As you listen to and silently recite the following rune, be aware that , you are emptying the directions of Sacred Space one after another around you, your out-breaths sending away all that is distracting, disturbing, stressful, and tense (See *Table1*, page 26).

Opening The Directions & Entering The Deep Peace

Spirit at centre,

Spirit below me,

Spirit above me,

Spirit before me,

Spirit behind me,

Spirit to my right side

Spirit to my left side,

Stream of Spirit through me, with me, and around me,

In the Name of the Stillness,

All be well!

You remain sitting or standing quietly, your breathing is

slow and steady.

With each outbreath the energies of

the directions are stilled.

A nutshell review of the relative coordinates will be useful here:

Centre: the Source, the Stillness, the core of being and centre of your self.

Below and Above: that which has the highest and deepest meaning for you.

Before: The potential of the future, your personal destiny, goals and aspirations.

Behind: the strength of the past, drawn from your experiences and ancestors.

Before: The potential of the future, your personal destiny, goals and aspirations.

Right Side: what you will give to a situation, your motivation.

Left Side: What you will take from a situation.

These essential meanings are extended and enhanced according to which cardinal direction you are facing. However, you don't need to consciously think about the directions for the method to work. You will have activated the far memory of their significance and power just by reading this folio.

Direction	Tension points
East	Thinking, Thoughts
South	Desires
West	Feelings
North	Sensations
Above	Aspiration, Ambition, Selfawareness, Egoic energies
Below	Shadow self, Depression, Drag of past
Centre	Force of one's Spirit,

Table1. Amongst much else, the directions relate to, and inter-connect with, various aspects or elements of our being as indicated in the table above. These are traditional significations of the Directions as they relate to the human soul

I have been in an uneasy chair
Above Caer Sidi,
And the whirling round
without motion
Between three elements
—Hanes Taliesin

The Oath:
The core of this was received word for word in my original dream. It married itself quite naturally in the final few lines to a poem I had previously written for my *Secrets of a Faery Landscape* (appearing on page 83 of that book).

"I bind myself ..."
When our Faery Other binds our hands together they are first joined by making a circle of our thumb and forefingers, ringing them together with those of our Faery Other. This gesture, of touching thumb and forefinger to make a circle with the remaining three fingers pointing up is an old gesture of Seership (one looks through the hole made by thumb and forefinger). It is also a ritual sign of Faery Friendship. It is useful to make this gesture before starting creative work. The triple cord is wound three (3x3) times around. All this can be ritually enacted.

"Sky, land and sea," "oak, ash and faery Tree" (thorn).
These are traditional oathing formulae in the Celtic Traditions.

The Emissary The Faery Child.

"The Thirteen Dreams": refers to the Great Faery presences that are universal types and appear in many traditions. They are closely connected to the cycles of time or rotations of energy known as the *thirteen* (or sometimes *nine) Faery Moons.*

"Bound together, Reborn forever" committed to the process of planetary transformation and spiritual regeneration destined to arise from a living covenant with Faery.

A Simple Ceremony

For connecting with & mediating the Presence of the Radiant Faery Child

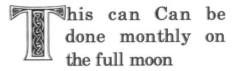his can Can be done monthly on the full moon

A special working of it may be done on or near the winter solstice and over the twelve days following total of 13 days-- a traditionally liminal period wherein the upcoming lunar year is magically contained and condensed. One day for each lunar period of the Thirteen Dreamers..

Items Needed:

- This description,
- a copy of the image on page 29,
- 1 candle,
- 3 tea lights.

Lay the image on you altar or other space for inner work, with the figure of Hound (the Quest Dreamer) closest to you.

A. Place your main candle on the image of the Quest) and the tea lights one on each of the glyphs of the sun which represent

1. The "conceiving of powers" which occurs at night below the horizon and in the UnderRealm.

2. The birth of the Radiant Faery Child ç solstice sunrise point.

3. of point of illumination ç noon or transit

B. Recite the following convocation which appears in my book *Secrets of a faery Landscape (Green Fire 2012)*

Now is the Time
Of the Gathering of Presences,
Of the sounding of the Harp,
Within the Well of Stars;

Of the singing of the Queen,
Her Faery song of Life;
Of the Green Fire of Faery,
Streaming from the Void.
Stars within Earth,
Earth within Stars,
Mortal and Immortal
Ringed together,
Reborn forever.
Peace to all Powers,
Light on all Ways,
In the Name of the Radiant
Child
of Faery,
Be All Well.

C. Light the three tea lights in succession from the flame of the main candle As these are lit recite the ritual rubrics below, meditating silently in between each one:

1. *Conceiving of Powers*
2. *Birth of the Radiant Child*

3. Illumination

D. Mediate the power and Light of the Child and the Apple star for as long as you will.

Notes On The Ceremony:

The Apple Star (*Winter Solstice 2012*)

Signifies the birth of the Radiant Faery Child in consciousness. This event is associated with the current speculations about the winter solstice of 2012. This is the alignment of the sun with the centre of the Milky Way, which in fact occurs every winter solstice over a period of approximately 245 years (roughly from winter solstice 1975 to Winter winter solstice 2220).

The pattern made on the land is that of a five-pointed star or Apple Star. This Apple Star is a secret stellar pattern reflected in the earth and UnderRealm. The lines signify streams of power occurring simultaneously in the Three Realms, activating influences and energies that may affect human consciousness in a profound way. Their pattern is dependent on the four Stars of Destiny and the triple solstice as viewed from Glastonbury Tor: It is not necessary to be in Somerset or even to

have visited the area to participate in this act of magico-spiritual communion and mediation.

―――――――――

About The Author

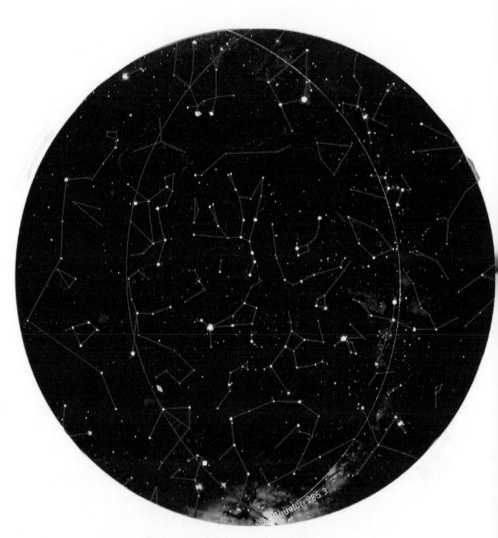

On the winter solstice of the Galactic alignment period (circa 1975-2020), the galactic equator and the Ecliptic form a Vesica Pisces in the sky over Glastonbury, Somerset.

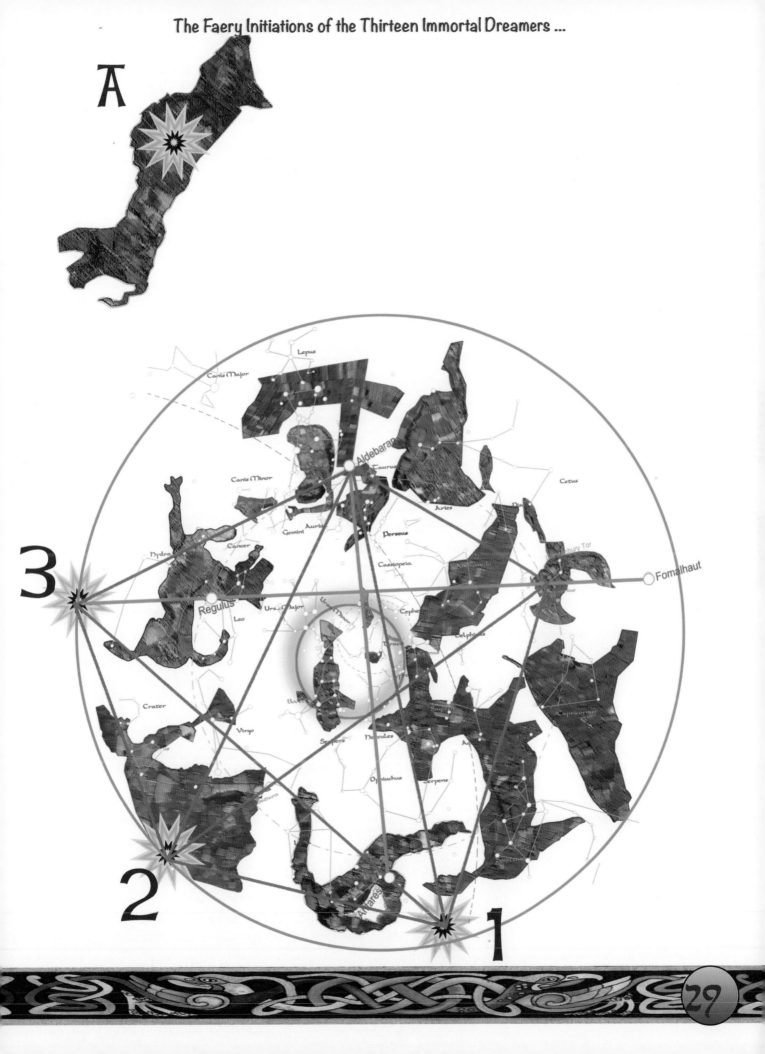

Coleston Brown enjoys a

simple life in the Irish countryside. He spends most of his free time quietly working on various projects designed to further the Faery-Human Covenant and the Magical Way.

www. magicalways.com

Picture Credits

Page 1, The !3 Dreamers. © 2007 by Coleston Brown

Pages2-32, Celtic Knot page runner © 1997 by Jessie Skillen.

Page 7, The Lion in the landscape, *the Cait Sidhe* © 2007 by Coleston Brown

Page 6 upper, after an engraving by Michael Maier in *Symbola Aureae Mensae duodecim nationum* (1617). (image in the public domain)

Page 6 lower, The Sleeping Shaman © 2013 by Coleston Brown

Page 8, The Grail Knight, Frederick J.Waugh ~ 1921 (image in the public domain

Page 9, Glastonbury Abbey Photo © 1997 by Jessie Skillen.

Page10, Encounter with a faery, George W. Russel (A.E.) ~ 1919 (image in the public domain).

Page 21, The Stone © 2007 by Coleston Brown

Page 13, Glastonbury Faery Swan. © 2012 by Jessie Skillen.

Page 14, upper, The Eight Daoist Immortals in their boat saiing the Heavens, from *The Mythology Of All Races* Volume Viii Edited by John Arnott Macculloch, 1928) (image in the public domain)

Page 14, lower, The Faery Ship © 2007 by Coleston Brown

Page 15, upper, The !3 Dreamers in the lanscape of Somerset. © 2007 by Coleston Brown

Page 15, lower, The !3 effigies in the lanscape of Somerset. 1934? by Katharine Maltwood, Photo © Coleston Brown 2008.

Page 18, The Havens © 2012 by Jessie Skillen.

Page 19, Salmon of Wisdom © 2007 by Coleston Brown.

Page 20, The Faery Hare of Glastonbury © 1997 by Jessie Skillen (painted on wood, *see also page 32*).

Page 24,The Horned Woman, Weaver of Destinies. © 2012 by Jessie Skillen.

Page 25,The Seven Directions. © 2010 by Coleston Brown

Page 26,Table of Directions and tension points. © 2012 by Coleston Brown

Page 27, Circular star background courtesy of The Sky astronomy program.

Page 28, On the winter solstice of the Galactic alignment period (circa 1975-2020), the galactic equator and the Ecliptic form a Vesica Pisces in the sky over Glastonbury, Somerset. (courtesy of The Sky astronomy program.

Page 29, The !3 Dreamers and The Apple Star in the landscape of Somerset. © 2007 by Coleston Brown

Page 30, Photo of the author in a Faery Glen, County Antrim. Photo 2011 by Jessie Skillen.

Page 31, Winter Solstice stellar alignments in the Glastonbury Landscape. © 2007 by Coleston Brown

Page 32, The Enchanted Hare in the landscape of the Glastonbury Faery Ring © 1997 by Jessie Skillen.

Power Alignments of Stellar Fire in the Glastonbury Enclosure. The three solstice points are A) Conceiving of powers, B) Sunrise/Birth, C) Transit/ Illumination.

Winter Solstice stellar alignments in the Glastonbury Landscape. © 2007 by Coleston Brown

The Enchanted Hare in the landscape of the
Glastonbury Faery Ring © 1997 by Jessie Skillen.

Printed in Great Britain
by Amazon

23918635R00021